Easy-to-Make Wooden Candlesticks, Chandeliers and Lamps

MEASURED DRAWINGS AND INSTRUCTIONS
FOR 14 TRADITIONAL PROJECTS

HENRY J. KAUFFMAN
Drawings by Gary R. Hague

Dover Publications, Inc., New York

Published in Canada by General Publishing Company, Ltd., 30 Lesmill Road, Don Mills, Toronto, Ontario.
Published in the United Kingdom by Constable and Company, Ltd., 10 Orange Street, London WC2H 7EG.

Easy-to-Make Wooden Candlesticks, Chandeliers and Lamps is a new work, first published by Dover Publications, Inc., in 1982.

Manufactured in the United States of America
Dover Publications, Inc.
180 Varick Street
New York, N.Y. 10014

Library of Congress Cataloging in Publication Data

Kauffman, Henry J., 1908–
    Easy-to-make wooden candlesticks, chandeliers, and lamps.

    1. Lamps. 2. Chandeliers. 3. Candlesticks. 4. Woodwork. I. Title.
TT197.5.L34K38   674'.88   81-19403
ISBN 0-486-24309-5   AACR2

Introduction

The practice of working with a lathe can be traced back to a remote period in history; early evidence of this craft has been found among Egyptian antiquities! It seems likely that the lathe originated when a splinter of bone or flint was attached to a short stick; rubbing the stick between the palms of the hands would give the tool a rotary motion.[1] The lathe has undergone a considerable metamorphosis since its humble beginning, and today learning how to work with a lathe is a natural progression in the development of the skills of a modern wood craftsman.

This volume has been written for the amateur woodworker with some lathe experience; it provides directions and measured drawings for fourteen lighting devices. These may be used as teaching projects and as beginning or practice projects for novice woodworkers. Although there are basic step-by-step instructions for completing each design, this book does not actually describe how to work with a lathe. There are many excellent books available for those interested in an in-depth study of turning.

Most of the designs in this book are traditional. However, there is a sprinkling of contemporary patterns for those who wish to work in that direction. The drawings accompanying these projects have been carefully labeled with exact measurements, but these measurements are merely suggestions. The drawings can be scaled up or down to make any size lighting device required.

The type of wood that is used may vary according to availability and choice of color and grain. Hardwoods such as birch, maple, walnut, cherry and mahogany are excellent choices. Poplar or pine can be used, although staining is recommended to improve the overall appearance; these woods are quite receptive to stain and will not need a filler. The open-grained woods such as walnut and mahogany will require a filler to provide a smooth finish; fillers can be purchased at most paint and hardware stores.

All turned work can be finished with French polish, varnish, shellac or lacquer. Check with your local hardware store for the many new commercially prepared and easy-to-use finishes that are available; follow the manufacturer's directions for use. Usually more than one finishing coat is necessary, with intermediate steps of sanding with steel wool or fine abrasive paper in between applications.

---

[1]John Jacob Holtzapffel, *Hand or Simple Turning: Principles and Practice* (1881; reprint ed., New York: Dover Publications, Inc., 1976), pp. 2–3.

1. Candlestick

1. Select the type and size of wood desired. Sketch measurement lines on wood following diagram.

2. Bore a $^{13}/_{16}$"-diameter $\times$ 1"-deep candle socket in perfect center of member; a forstner bit is suggested for boring end grain.

3. Install wood member in lathe; allow lathe center to run in socket or plug opening to accept lathe center.

4. Turn member to round.

5. Establish finished diameters at several points of member; check with outside calipers.

6. Turn to finished contours.

7. Smooth with abrasive paper.

8. Raise grain by dampening with water; smooth again for final finish.

9. Apply desired finish while project is in lathe.

10. Remove finished candlestick from lathe.

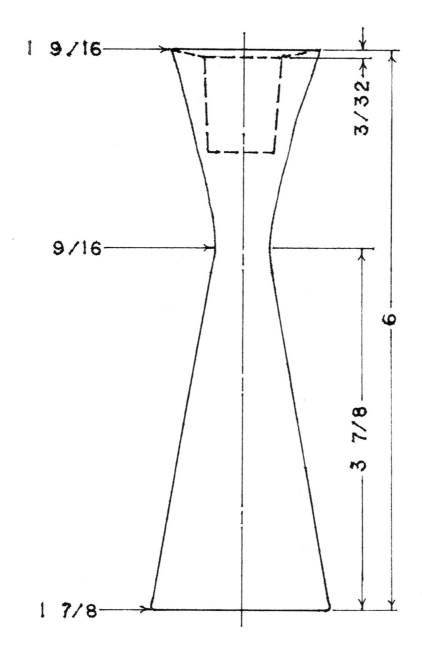

1 9/16

3/32

9/16

6

3 7/8

1 7/8

2. Candlestick

1. Select the type and size of wood desired. Sketch measurement lines on wood following diagram.

2. Bore a $^{13}/_{16}$"-diameter × 1"-deep candle socket in perfect center of member; a forstner bit is suggested for boring end grain.

3. Install wood member in lathe; allow lathe center to run in socket or plug opening to accept lathe center.

4. Turn member to round.

5. Establish finished diameters at several points of member; check with outside calipers.

6. Turn to finished contours.

7. Smooth with abrasive paper.

8. Raise grain by dampening with water; smooth again for final finish.

9. Apply desired finish while project is in lathe.

10. Remove finished candlestick from lathe.

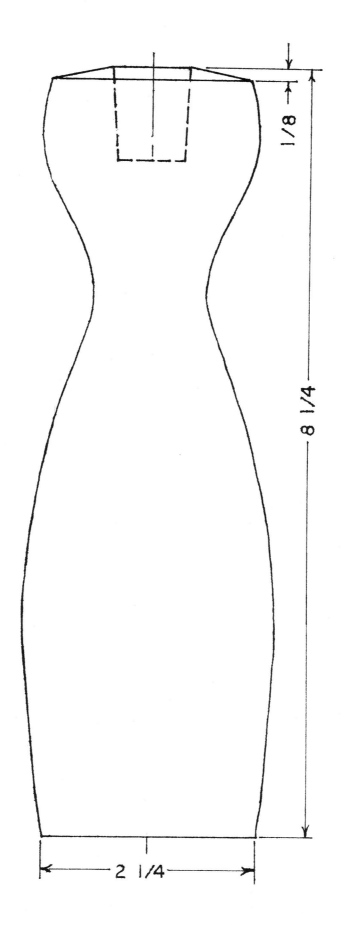

1/8

8 1/4

2 1/4

3. Candlestick

1. Select the type and size of wood desired. Sketch measurement lines on vertical and base members following diagram.

2. Bore a $^{13}\!/_{16}$"-diameter $\times$ 1"-deep candle socket in perfect center of vertical member; a forstner bit is suggested for boring end grain.

3. Install vertical member in lathe; allow lathe center to run in socket or plug opening to accept lathe center. Turn tenon at end opposite socket.

4. Attach base member to faceplate; turn mortise to fit tenon.

5. Glue joint and clamp in lathe overnight.

6. Turn both members to round.

7. Cut narrow slits to major diameters; check with outside calipers.

8. Turn precisely to size and smooth with abrasive paper.

9. Raise grain by dampening with water; smooth again for final finish.

10. Apply desired finish while project is in lathe.

11. Remove finished candlestick from lathe.

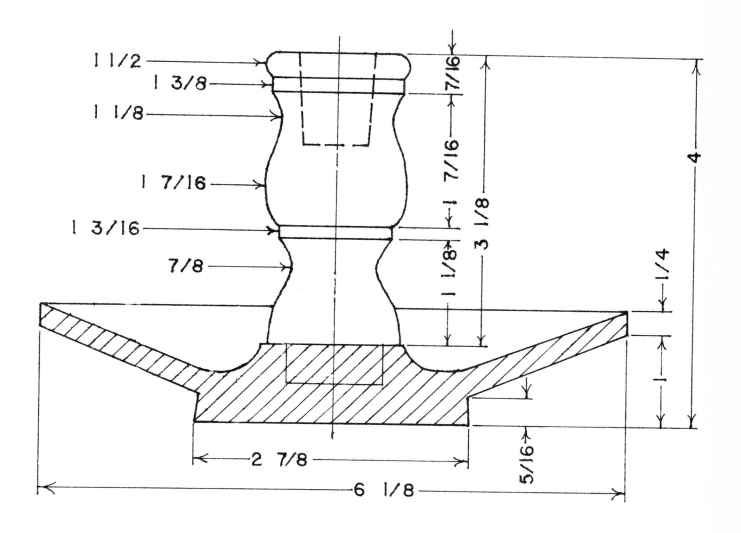

1 1/2

1 3/8

1 1/8

1 7/16

1 3/16

7/8

7/16

1 7/16

3 1/8

1 1/8

4

1/4

1

5/16

2 7/8

6 1/8

9

4. Candlestick

Shown on the front cover.

1. Select the type and size of wood desired. Sketch measurement lines on vertical and base members following diagram.

2. Bore a $^{13}\!/_{16}$"-diameter × 1"-deep candle socket in perfect center of vertical member; a forstner bit is suggested for boring end grain.

3. Install vertical member in lathe; allow lathe center to run in socket or plug opening to accept lathe center. Turn tenon at end opposite socket.

4. Attach base member to faceplate; turn mortise to fit tenon.

5. Glue joint and clamp in lathe overnight.

6. Turn both members to round.

7. Cut narrow slits to major diameters; check with outside calipers.

8. Turn precisely to size and smooth with abrasive paper.

9. Raise grain by dampening with water; smooth again for final finish.

10. Apply desired finish while project is in lathe.

11. Remove finished candlestick from lathe.

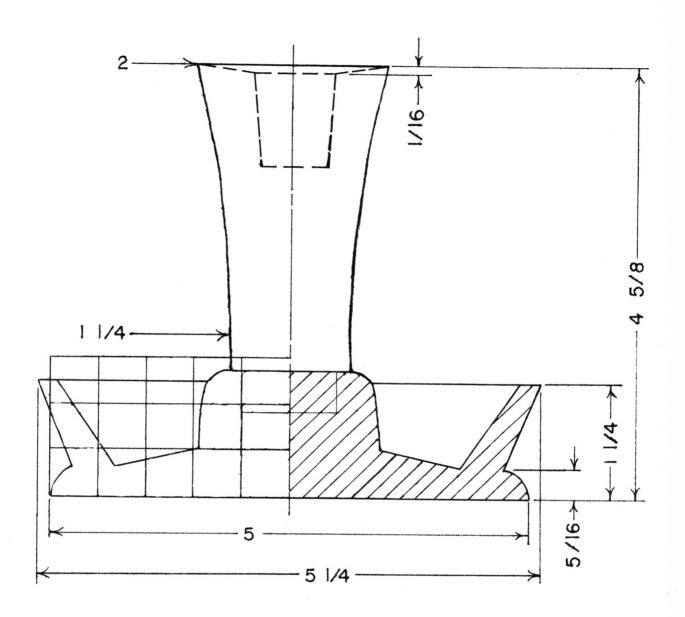

2

1/16

1 1/4

4 5/8

1 1/4

5/16

5

5 1/4

5. Candlestick

Shown on the front cover.

1. Select the type and size of wood desired. Sketch measurement lines on vertical and base members following diagram.

2. Bore a $^{13}/_{16}$"-diameter × 1"-deep candle socket in perfect center of vertical member; a forstner bit is suggested for boring end grain.

3. Install vertical member in lathe; allow lathe center to run in socket or plug opening to accept lathe center. Turn tenon at end opposite socket.

4. Attach base member to faceplate; turn mortise to fit tenon.

5. Glue joint and clamp in lathe overnight.

6. Turn both members to round.

7. Cut narrow slits to major diameters; check with outside calipers.

8. Turn precisely to size and smooth carefully with abrasive paper to retain details.

9. Raise grain by dampening with water; smooth again for final finish.

10. Apply desired finish while project is in lathe.

11. Remove finished candlestick from lathe.

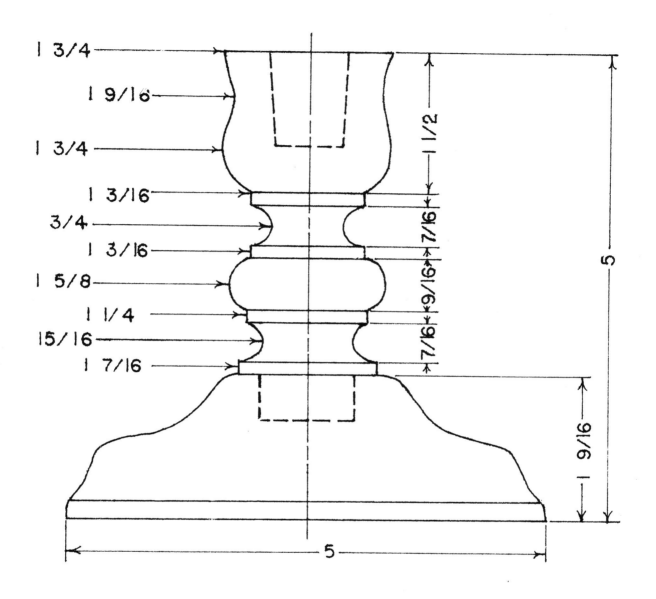

1 3/4

1 9/16

1 3/4

1 3/16

3/4

1 3/16

1 5/8

1 1/4

15/16

1 7/16

1 1/2

7/16

9/16

7/16

5

1 9/16

5

NOTE: ALL SHOULDERS 1/8 INCH

6. Candlestick

Shown on the front cover.

1. Select the type and size of wood desired. Sketch measurement lines on vertical and base members following diagram.

2. Bore a $^{13}/_{16}$"-diameter × 1"-deep candle socket in perfect center of vertical member; a forstner bit is suggested for boring end grain.

3. Install vertical member in lathe; allow lathe center to run in socket or plug opening to accept lathe center. Turn tenon at end opposite socket.

4. Attach base member to faceplate; turn mortise to fit tenon.

5. Glue joint and clamp in lathe overnight.

6. Turn both members to round.

7. Cut narrow slits to major diameters; check with outside calipers.

8. Turn precisely to size and smooth carefully with abrasive paper to retain details.

9. Raise grain by dampening with water; smooth again for final finish.

10. Apply desired finish while project is in lathe.

11. Remove finished candlestick from lathe.

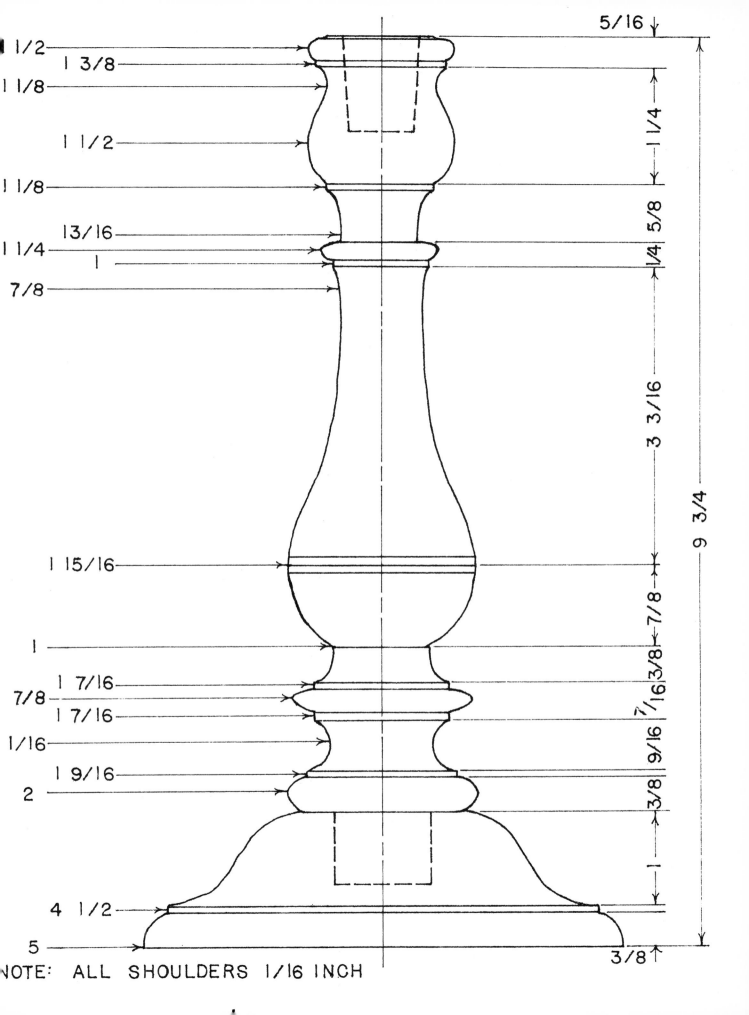

5/16

1/2

1 3/8

1 1/8

1 1/2

1 1/8

13/16

1 1/4

1

7/8

1 15/16

1

1 7/16

7/8

1 7/16

1/16

1 9/16

2

4 1/2

5

1 1/4

5/8

1/4

3 3/16

9 3/4

7/8

3/8

7/16

9/16

3/8

1

3/8

NOTE: ALL SHOULDERS 1/16 INCH

7. Lamp Base

1. Select the type and size of wood desired. Sketch measurement lines on vertical and base members following diagram.

2. Before inserting vertical member in lathe, a hole must be drilled to accommodate the wire. Bore a ⅜"-diameter hole (starting from each end) in perfect center of vertical member.

3. Plug holes to accept lathe centers.

4. Install vertical member in lathe; turn tenon.

5. Attach base member to faceplate; turn mortise to fit tenon.

6. Glue joint and clamp in lathe overnight.

7. Turn both members to round.

8. Cut major diameters on vertical member; check with outside calipers.

9. Turn vertical member precisely to size and smooth with abrasive paper.

10. Turn base member precisely to size and smooth with abrasive paper.

11. Raise grain by dampening with water; smooth again for final finish.

12. Apply desired finish while project is in lathe.

13. Remove finished lamp base from lathe.

14. Drill center hole in base to accommodate the wire; countersink center hole. Use ¼" drill to cut channel for wire from center hole to side edge of base.

15. Purchase a lamp-wiring kit with all necessary lamp parts from a hardware or lamp store; read manufacturer's directions for assembly.

16. Wire lamp following manufacturer's directions.

17. Fit with appropriate shade.

1/8 INCH PIPE NIPPLE × 2 1/2 INCHES

3/4

2 15/16

3/8

1 5/8

12 1/4

8 1/2

13 3/4

3/8 DRILL

2 15/16

3/8

1 1/2

6

1/4 DRILL

3/4 DRILL

8. Lamp Base

Shown on the front cover.

1. Select the type and size of wood desired. Sketch measurement lines on vertical and base members following diagram.

2. Before inserting vertical member in lathe, a hole must be drilled to accommodate the wire. Bore a ⅜"-diameter hole (starting from each end) in perfect center of vertical member.

3. Plug holes to accept lathe centers.

4. Install vertical member in lathe; turn tenon.

5. Attach base member to faceplate; turn mortise to fit tenon.

6. Glue joint and clamp in lathe overnight.

7. Turn both members to round.

8. Cut major diameters on vertical member; check with outside calipers.

9. Turn vertical member precisely to size and smooth with abrasive paper.

10. Turn base member precisely to size and smooth with abrasive paper.

11. Raise grain by dampening with water; smooth again for final finish.

12. Apply desired finish while project is in lathe.

13. Remove finished lamp base from lathe.

14. Drill center hole in base to accommodate the wire; countersink center hole. Use ¼" drill to cut channel for wire from center hole to side edge of base.

15. Purchase a lamp-wiring kit with all necessary lamp parts from a hardware or lamp store; read manufacturer's directions for assembly.

16. Wire lamp following manufacturer's directions.

17. Fit with appropriate shade.

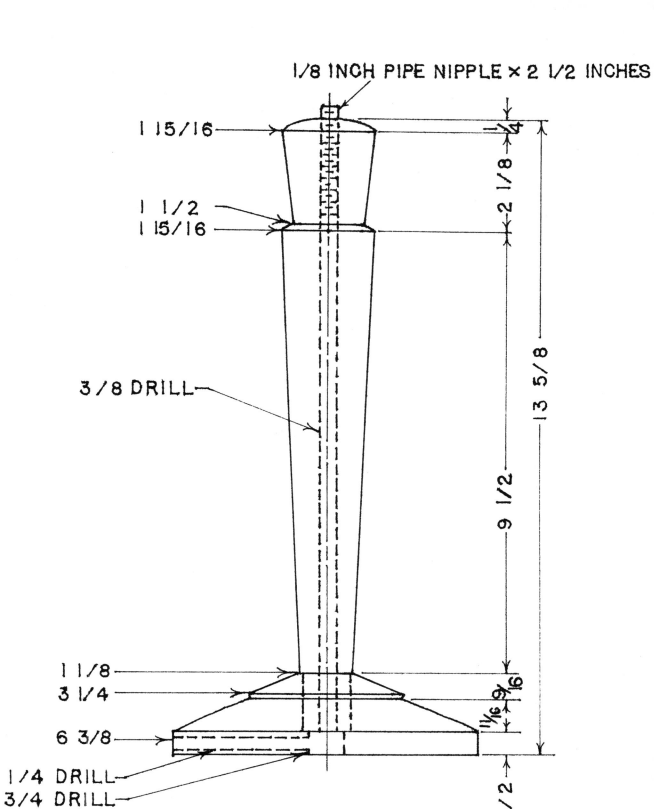

1/8 INCH PIPE NIPPLE × 2 1/2 INCHES

1 15/16

1 1/2
1 15/16

3/8 DRILL

1 1/8
3 1/4
6 3/8

1/4 DRILL
3/4 DRILL

1/4
2 1/8

13 5/8

9 1/2

9/16
1 1/16

1/2

9. Lamp Base

1. Select the type and size of wood desired. Sketch measurement lines on vertical and base members following diagram.

2. Before inserting vertical member in lathe, a hole must be drilled to accommodate the wire. Bore a ⅜"-diameter hole (starting from each end) in perfect center of vertical member.

3. Plug holes to accept lathe centers.

4. Install vertical member in lathe; turn tenon.

5. Attach base member to faceplate; turn mortise to fit tenon.

6. Glue joint and clamp in lathe overnight.

7. Turn both members to round.

8. Cut major diameters on vertical member; check with outside calipers.

9. Turn vertical member precisely to size and smooth carefully with abrasive paper to retain details.

10. Turn base member precisely to size and smooth carefully with abrasive paper to retain details.

11. Raise grain by dampening with water; smooth again for final finish.

12. Apply desired finish while project is in lathe.

13. Remove finished lamp base from lathe.

14. Drill center hole in base to accommodate the wire; countersink center hole. Use ¼" drill to cut channel for wire from center hole to side edge of base.

15. Purchase a lamp-wiring kit with all necessary lamp parts from a hardware or lamp store; read manufacturer's directions for assembly.

16. Wire lamp following manufacturer's directions.

17. Fit with appropriate shade.

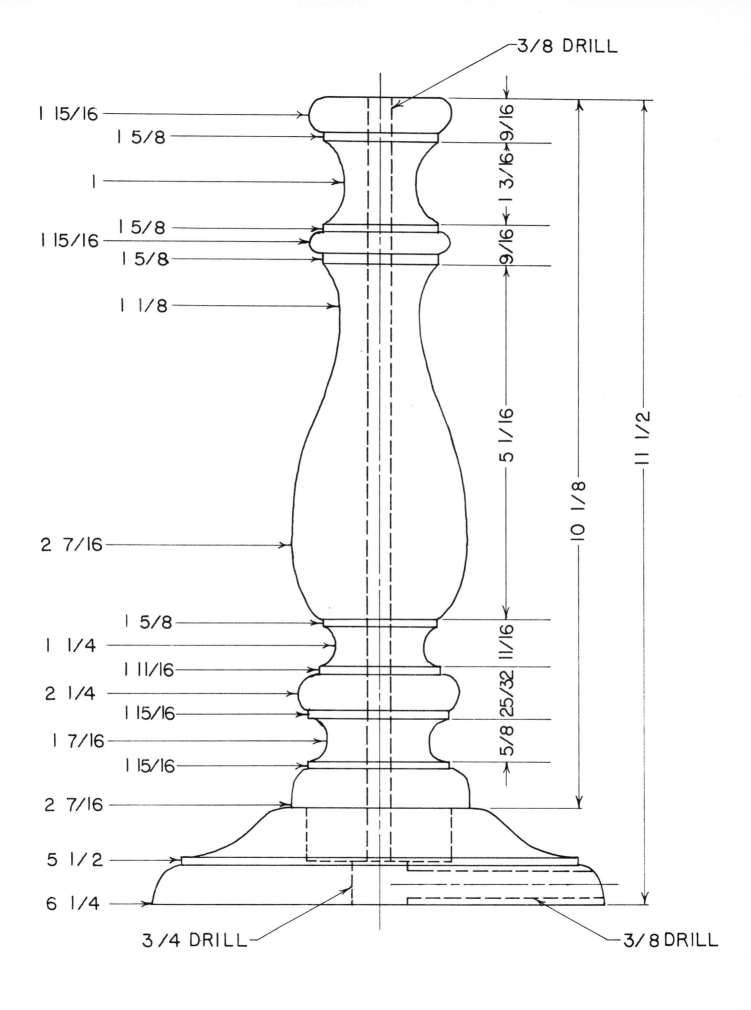

3/8 DRILL

1 15/16

1 5/8

1

1 5/8

1 15/16

1 5/8

1 1/8

9/16

1 3/16

9/16

5 1/16

2 7/16

10 1/8

11 1/2

1 5/8

1 1/4

1 11/16

2 1/4

11/16

1 15/16

1 7/16

25/32

1 15/16

5/8

2 7/16

5 1/2

6 1/4

3/4 DRILL

3/8 DRILL

10. Lamp Base

1. Select the type and size of wood desired. Sketch measurement lines on vertical and base members following diagram.

2. Before inserting vertical member in lathe, a hole must be drilled to accommodate the wire. Bore a ⅜″-diameter hole (starting from each end) in perfect center of vertical member.

3. Plug holes to accept lathe centers.

4. Install vertical member in lathe; turn tenon.

5. Attach base member to faceplate; turn mortise to fit tenon.

6. Glue joint and clamp in lathe overnight.

7. Turn both members to round.

8. Cut major diameters on vertical member; check with outside calipers.

9. Turn vertical member precisely to size and smooth carefully with abrasive paper to retain details.

10. Turn base member precisely to size and smooth carefully with abrasive paper to retain details.

11. Raise grain by dampening with water; smooth again for final finish.

12. Apply desired finish while project is in lathe.

13. Remove finished lamp base from lathe.

14. Drill center hole in base to accommodate the wire; countersink center hole. Use ¼″ drill to cut channel for wire from center hole to side edge of base.

15. Purchase a lamp-wiring kit with all necessary lamp parts from a hardware or lamp store; read manufacturer's directions for assembly.

16. Wire lamp following manufacturer's directions.

17. Fit with appropriate shade.

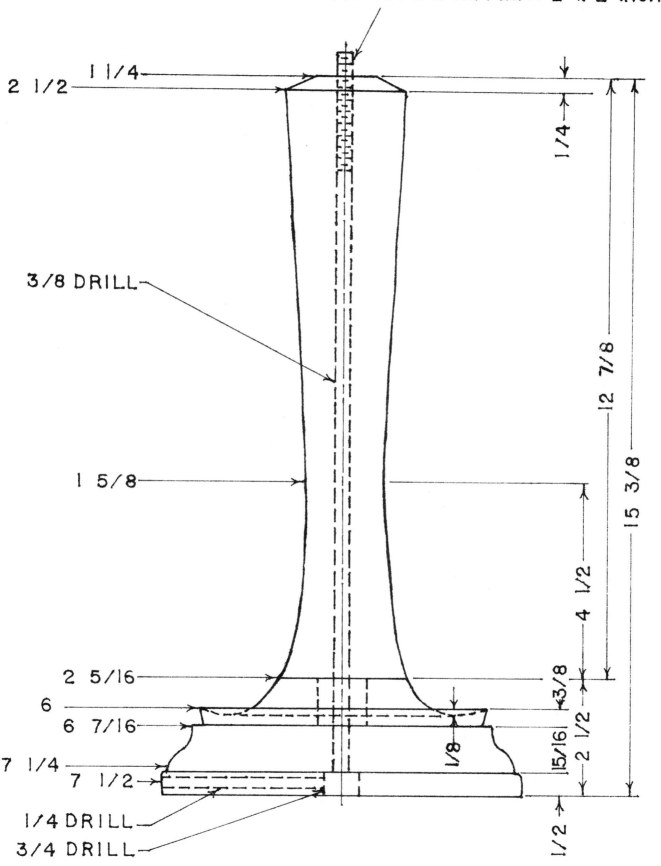

1/8 INCH PIPE NIPPLE × 2 1/2 INCHES

1 1/4

2 1/2

3/8 DRILL

1/4

12 7/8

15 3/8

1 5/8

4 1/2

4

2 5/16

3/8

6

15/16

6 7/16

1/8

2 1/2

7 1/4

7 1/2

1/4 DRILL

3/4 DRILL

1/2

23

11. Lamp Base

1. Select the type and size of wood desired (to economize wood, use stock about 4½″ square for vertical member). Sketch measurement lines on vertical and base members following diagram.

2. Before inserting vertical member in lathe, a hole must be drilled to accommodate the wire. Bore a ⅜″-diameter hole (starting from each end) in perfect center of vertical member.

3. Plug holes to accept lathe centers.

4. Install vertical member in lathe; turn tenon.

5. Attach base member to faceplate; turn mortise to fit tenon.

6. Glue joint and clamp in lathe overnight.

7. Turn both members to round.

8. Cut major diameters on vertical member; check with outside calipers.

9. Turn vertical member precisely to size and smooth with abrasive paper, being careful to retain "rounds" and "flats."

10. Turn base member precisely to size and smooth with abrasive paper.

11. Raise grain by dampening with water; smooth again for final finish.

12. Apply desired finish while project is in lathe.

13. Remove finished lamp base from lathe.

14. Drill center hole in base to accommodate the wire; countersink center hole. Use ¼″ drill to cut channel for wire from center hole to side edge of base.

15. Purchase a lamp-wiring kit with all necessary lamp parts from a hardware or lamp store; read manufacturer's directions for assembly.

16. Wire lamp following manufacturer's directions.

17. Fit with appropriate shade.

1/8 INCH PIPE NIPPLE × 2 1/2 INCHES

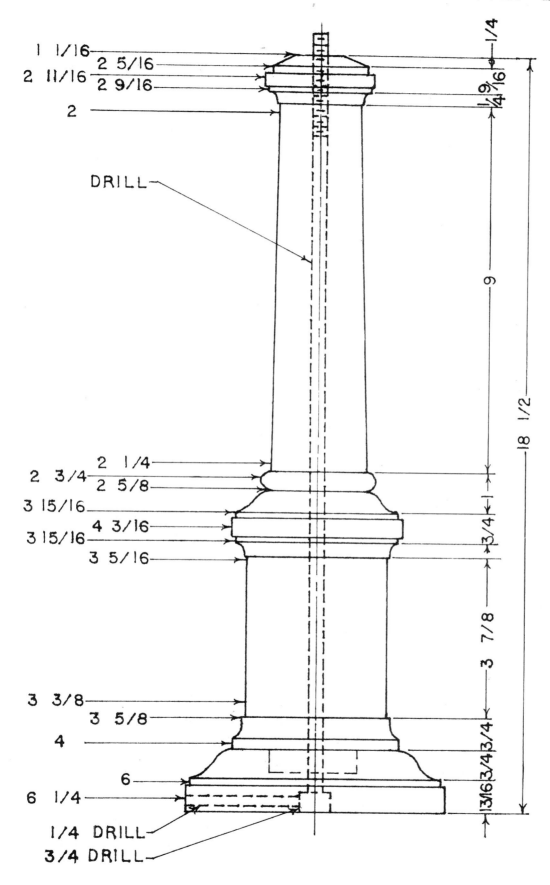

1 1/16
2 5/16
2 11/16
2 9/16
2

DRILL

1/4
9/16
4 1/4

9

18 1/2

2 1/4
2 3/4
2 5/8
3 15/16
4 3/16
3 15/16
3 5/16

1
3/4

3 7/8

3 3/8
3 5/8
4

6
6 1/4

1/4 DRILL
3/4 DRILL

13/16 3/4 3/4

12. Three-Arm Sconce

Shown on the front cover.
(Directions are given for a pair of sconces.)

1. Select the type of wood desired; you will need two pieces, each 2⅞" × 1⁷⁄₁₆" × 13" for vertical member parts, ½" × 1¼" × 27" wood for arms, and 3"-diameter rounds for candle cups and saucers.

2. Glue two vertical member parts together, inserting a piece of paper between the two parts so they can be separated after turning. Sketch measurement lines on glued member following diagram.

3. Install vertical member in lathe and turn to round.

4. Establish finished diameters at several points of member; check with outside calipers.

5. Turn to finished contours.

6. Smooth with abrasive paper.

7. Raise grain by dampening with water; smooth again for final finish.

8. Remove from lathe. Separate vertical member parts by inserting a chisel carefully between the glued pieces.

9. Drill hole in back of each vertical member part and apply metal tab for hanging.

10. Turn six candle cups and six saucers to sizes indicated (see detail on page 32); smooth same as vertical member. Bore a candle socket in perfect center of each candle cup.

11. Cut six 4½"-long arms out of ½" × 1¼" wood; use coping saw or jig-saw to shape a 1¼"-diameter base at one end of each arm as shown on left side of top diagram. Smooth each arm with abrasive paper, rounding corners with a file.

12. Measure and mark positions for three arms on each vertical member part; bore holes to correct size.

13. Glue arms to vertical member parts.

14. Attach candle cup and saucer to base end of each arm with a screw as shown.

15. Apply desired finish.

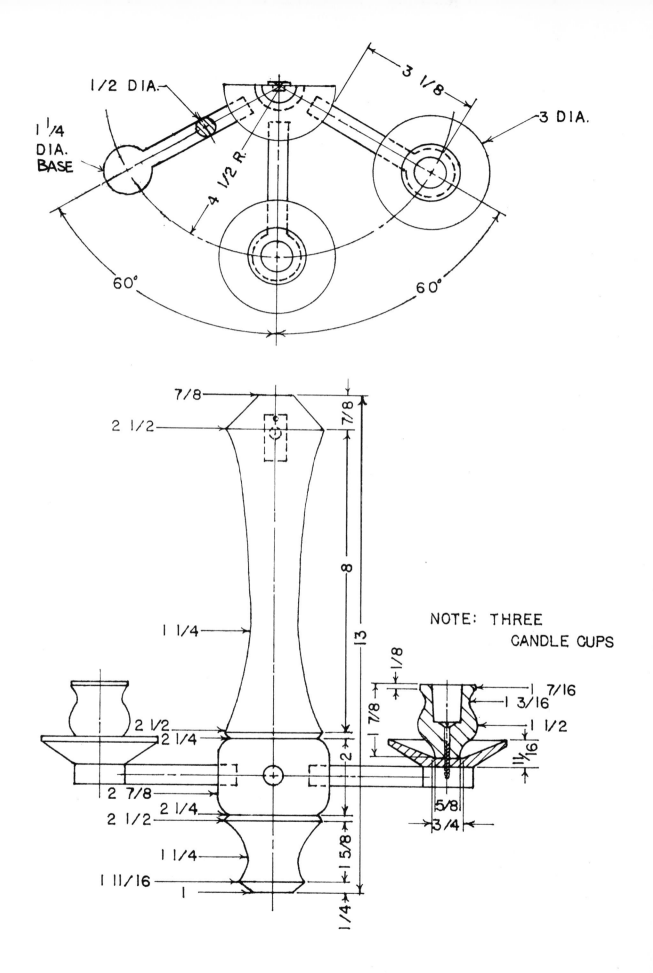

1/2 DIA.

1 1/4 DIA. BASE

3 1/8

3 DIA.

4 1/2 R.

60°   60°

7/8

2 1/2

7/8

8

13

1 1/4

2 1/2

2 1/4

2 7/8

2 1/4

2 1/2

1 1/4

1 11/16

1

2

1 5/8

1/4

NOTE: THREE CANDLE CUPS

1/8

7/8

1 7/16

1 3/16

1 1/2

1 1/16

5/8

3/4

27

13. Four-Arm Chandelier

Shown on the back cover.

1. Select the type and size of wood desired. Sketch measurement lines on vertical member following diagram.

2. Install vertical member in lathe and turn to round.

3. Establish finished diameters at several points of member; check with outside calipers.

4. Turn vertical member precisely to size and smooth with abrasive paper.

5. Measure, mark and cut mortises.

6. Raise grain by dampening with water; smooth again for final finish.

7. Enlarge pattern for arm to full size following diagram (each square = ½"). Cut four arms from ¾" wood using coping saw or jigsaw; cut tenons to fit mortises.

8. Turn four candle cups and four saucers to sizes indicated (see detail on page 32); smooth same as vertical member. Bore a candle socket in perfect center of each candle cup.

9. Glue arms to vertical member.

10. Attach candle cup and saucer to end of each arm with a screw as shown.

11. Apply desired finish.

12. Install screw eye for hanging.

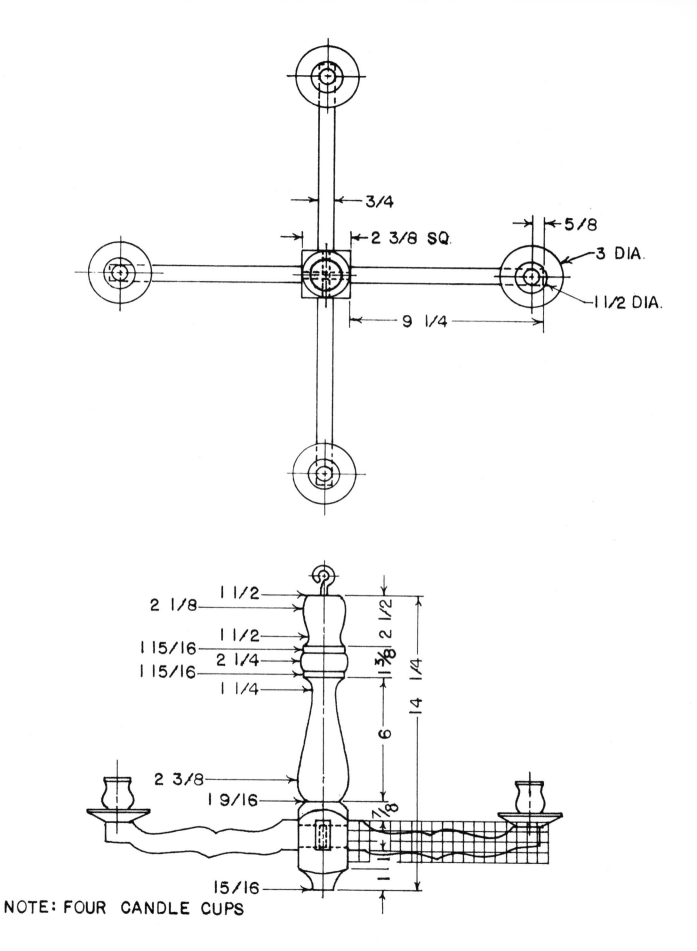

3/4

2 3/8 SQ.

5/8

3 DIA.

1 1/2 DIA.

9 1/4

1 1/2
2 1/8
1 1/2
1 15/16
2 1/4
1 15/16
1 1/4

2 1/2

1 3/8

14 1/4

6

2 3/8

1 9/16

7/8

15/16

NOTE: FOUR CANDLE CUPS

14. Six-Arm Chandelier

1. Select the type of wood desired; you will need one piece 3½"-square × 12" for vertical member, two ½" × 5½"-square pieces for base, ½" × 1½" × 48" length of wood for arms and 3"-diameter rounds for candle cups and saucers.

2. Cut two 4¾" hexagons from ½" × 5½"-square wood.

3. Cut six 8"-long arms out of ½" × 1½" wood; use coping saw or jigsaw to shape a 1½"-diameter base at one end of each arm as shown in diagram at lower right.

4. Measure, mark and cut six ¼"-deep channels in each hexagon to accept arms; channels in each hexagon must match perfectly!

5. Turn candle cups and saucers to sizes indicated; bore a candle socket in perfect center of each candle cup.

6. Plane vertical member into a 2½" hexagon as shown in diagrams on pages 31 and 32.

7. Smooth all parts with abrasive paper.

8. Raise grain by dampening with water; smooth again for final finish.

9. Insert and glue arms into one hexagon; glue hexagons together.

10. Attach cup and saucer to base end of each arm with a screw as shown.

11. Attach vertical member to hexagon base with two large screws.

12. Apply desired finish.

13. Install screw eye for hanging.

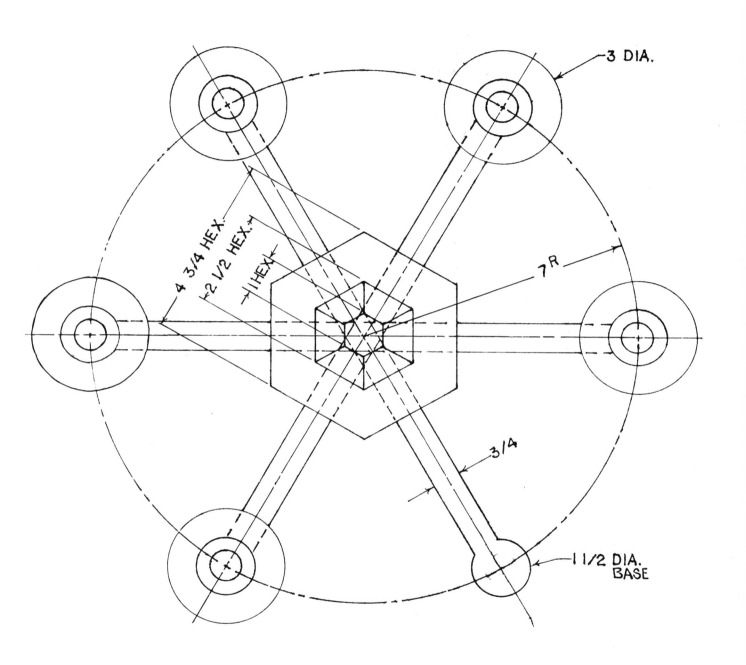

3 DIA.

4 3/4 HEX.

2 1/2 HEX.

1 HEX.

7 R

3/4

1 1/2 DIA.
BASE

See page 32 for additional diagrams.

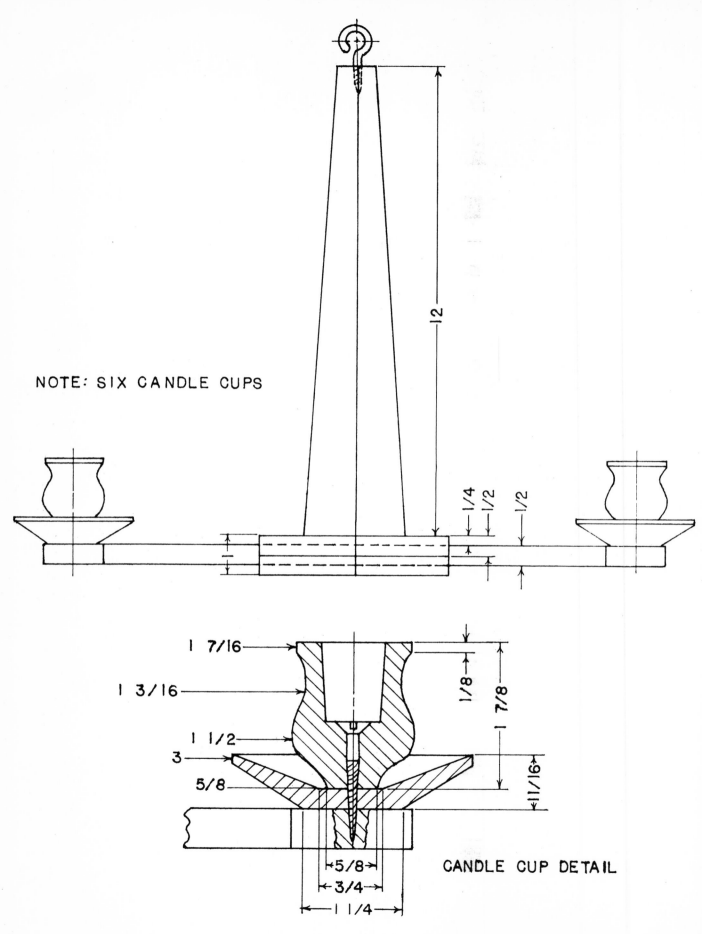

NOTE: SIX CANDLE CUPS

12

1/4
1/2
1/2

CANDLE CUP DETAIL

1 7/16
1 3/16
1 1/2
3
5/8

1/8
1 7/8
11/16

5/8
3/4
1 1/4

32